THE
J.W. LONGABERGER
COLLECTION

THE
J.W. LONGABERGER
COLLECTION™

Presented by **The LONGABERGER® COMPANY** *and* **TIME LIFE CUSTOM PUBLISHING**

© 1994 The Longaberger® Company

All rights reserved. No part of this book may be reproduced in any form or by any electronic or mechanical means, including information storage and retrieval devices or systems, without prior written permission from the publisher, except that brief passages may be quoted for reviews.
First printing. Printed in U.S.A.

Questions related to contents and distribution should be directed to your local Longaberger Consultant, or to Longaberger Customer Referral:

1-800-966-0374

The Longaberger Company
95 North Chestnut Street
Dresden, Ohio 43821-9600

J.W. COLLECTION, LONGABERGER BASKETS and LONGABERGER POTTERY are registered trademarks of The Longaberger Company.

TIME-LIFE is a registered trademark of Time Warner Inc. U.S.A.

THE LONGABERGER COMPANY

Chairman of the Board and Chief Executive Officer	Dave Longaberger
President	Tami Longaberger Kaido
Chief Operating Officer	Rachel Longaberger Schmidt
Vice President, Marketing and Sales	Betty Palm
Executive Director of Marketing	Jim Mannion
Director of Sales Development	Pam Herbert
Publications Manager	Rob Mosbacher
Senior Graphic Designer	Kate Williard

With special thanks to members of the Longaberger family:
Bonnie Longaberger
Genevieve Longaberger Hard
Wendy Longaberger Little
Jerry Longaberger
Larry Longaberger
Dave Longaberger
Rich Longaberger
Mary Ann Longaberger McCafferty
Judy Longaberger Swope
Ginny Lou Longaberger Wilcox
Gary Longaberger
Carmen Longaberger Fortney
Jeff Longaberger

Time-Life Books is a division of TIME LIFE INCORPORATED
President and Chief Executive Officer	John M. Fahey, Jr.
President, Time-Life Books	John D. Hall

TIME-LIFE CUSTOM PUBLISHING

Vice President and Publisher	Terry Newell
Director of Custom Publishing	Frances C. Mangan
Editorial Director	Robert A. Doyle
Operations Manager	Phyllis A. Gardner
Production Manager	Prudence G. Harris
Manager, New Business Development	Becky Wheeler

The J.W. Longaberger Collection, written by Rob Mosbacher, was produced for The Longaberger Company and Time-Life Custom Publishing by ST. REMY PRESS

Principal photography by Ron Levine, assisted by Marie Deruaz; except pps. 5, 6, 11, 13, 15, 17, 19, 21, 52, 53, 54 left, 58, 61 and 66

Special thanks to the Cherry Valley Lodge, Newark, Ohio

John Wendell Longaberger,
circa 1920

Foreword

Growing up in Dresden was the best time of my life, which I credit entirely to Mom and Dad. As the fifth of their 12 children, I remember that we, like any family, had our struggles. But doing without the bicycles, roller skates and new clothes that other kids had never mattered to us. Despite our hardships, we had pride. And Dad and Mom were good at helping us to turn fears into sources of laughter.

Mom and Dad provided powerful training, not so much in what they said as in what they did. They taught us the value of an honest day's work. They gave us freedom as long as we behaved ourselves and acted responsibly. And because they never showed any favoritism, we learned to stick together.

The J.W. Longaberger Collection was begun in 1983 as a tribute to Dad and Mom, a way to offer other families a little something of what they gave to us. At the time, I had no idea this special series of Dad's original baskets, which were such a big part of our lives, would become the valuable collectibles they are today. I shouldn't be surprised. Everything associated with Mom and Dad is worth treasuring and will never be out of style.

Thank you, Dad. Thank you, Mom. For so much. For everything.

—Dave Longaberger

Dresden's Main Street in the 1930s.

Dave Longaberger in his youth.

Bonnie Longaberger with son Dave at his farm.

The J.W. Longaberger Collection

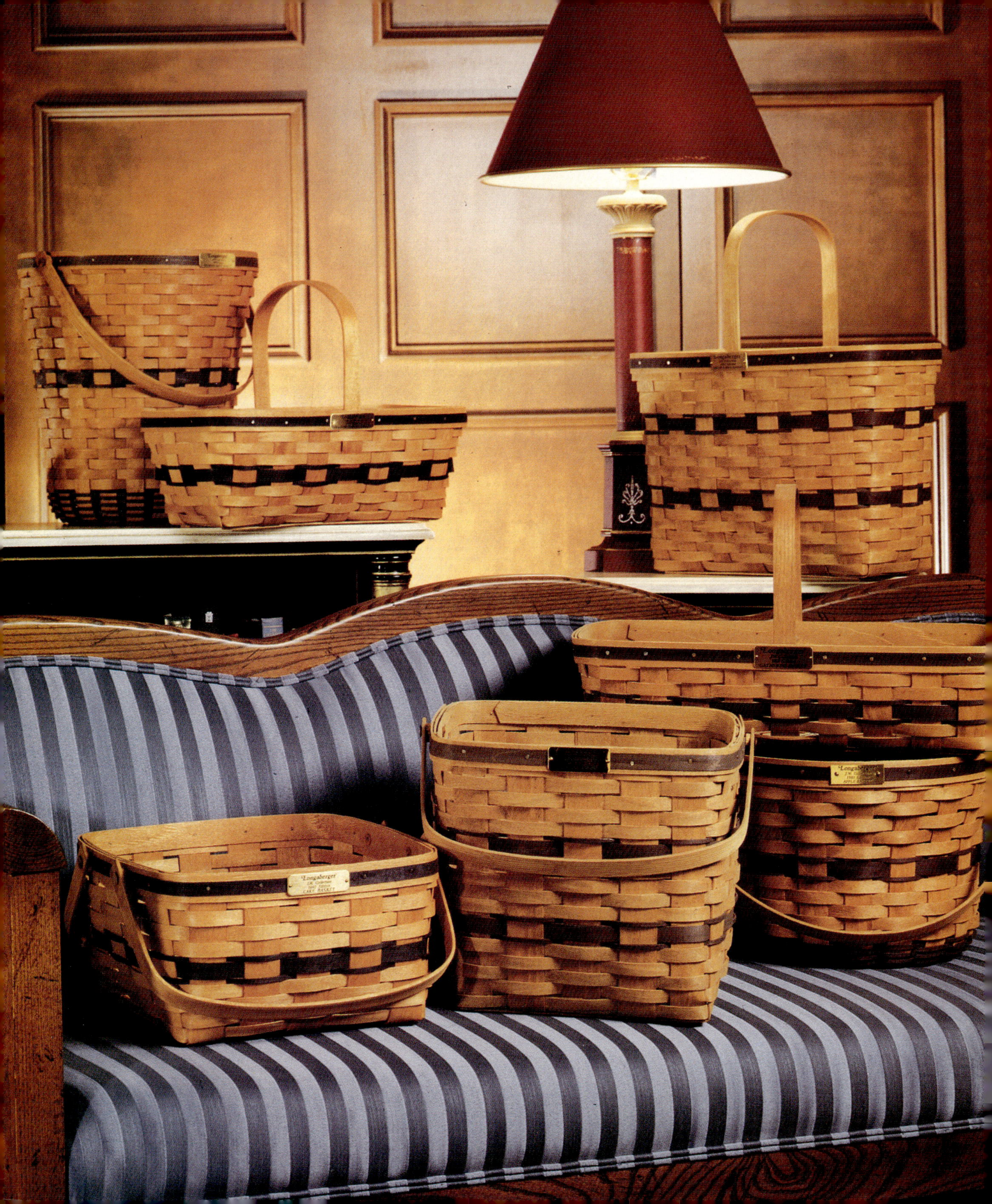
Longaberger

The beginnings of a legacy

On a sunny morning in 1948, Dresden, Ohio, is alive with foot traffic. As farmers, merchants and townspeople go about their daily errands, a simply-dressed woman moves from shop to shop, clutching in one hand a woven shopping basket and in the other the hand of her youngest son. She loads up her basket with fresh milk, eggs, fruits and vegetables, then turns a corner and stops for a visit in the backyard of a friend. The friend doesn't miss a beat as she hangs out her laundry. Chatting contentedly, she draws socks, shirts, and linens out of her well-worn laundry basket and pins them on the line.

Meanwhile, a boy rides down Main Street with a loaf of bread bouncing in a woven wooden basket on the front of his bicycle. Inside the bank, a customer drops a scrap of paper in a handwoven waste basket at the teller's counter. A farmer on a street corner peddles produce from bushel baskets made with inverted bottoms to help keep food fresh. In the shade of a tree at the river's edge, a couple enjoys a leisurely lunch carried from home in a graceful, handwoven picnic basket. That evening, women will carry layer cakes to a church social, delivering them moist and fresh in deep, square baskets trimmed with braids of paper twine.

A familiar feature in this scene from a bygone era was the wide variety of handmade, hardwood baskets. They were everywhere in a time before cardboard and plastics became commonplace—an essential thread of the fabric of life.

And baskets were particularly plentiful in this eastern Ohio village as the middle of the century approached. Most of them were made by a local master craftsman named John Wendell Longaberger, a man well known and respected by his neighbors. From the time he was a

THE J.W. LONGABERGER COLLECTION

John Wendell Longaberger (left) and Bonnie Jean Gist, 1927.

teenager until the last months of his life, J.W., as most people called him, worked his magic with hardwood splints, weaving baskets with discipline, care and pride. His baskets endured for decades and were handed down from one generation to the next. J.W.'s baskets came as close as anything to defining the community in which he lived. They also defined his family and a whole way of life—not just for his time, but for all time.

Seventeen-year-old Bonnie Jean Gist of Trinway, Ohio, didn't get a good look at the man behind the wheel of the old Ford touring car, but she didn't like the sound of his deep, mumbling voice. And even when she finally got a good look at J.W., she wasn't exactly swept off her feet. "I was raised with five boys," she later recalled. "Another one didn't excite me at all."

Little did she know that this would be the man with whom she would spend the next 45 years of her life. Much of that time she devoted to rais-

The J.W. Longaberger Collection

ing their 12 children in a house on Eighth Street in Dresden. And Bonnie certainly had no idea that Wendell, as she called him, would become the country's best known and most celebrated weaver of hardwood baskets.

In 1896, six years before their son J.W. was born, John and Carrie Longaberger had moved south from Niles, Ohio, to the small farming community of Dresden. At the age of 17, J.W. left high school to work alongside his father at the Dresden Basket Factory, a local business owned by a man named Guy Ryan.

At the Dresden Basket Factory, J.W. learned the craft of basket making and proved to be a gifted weaver. He took great pride and pleasure in his work, skillfully making large, round baskets with inverted bottoms for the pottery industry. Used to transport materials to and from the kilns and to ship finished ware, the sturdy baskets served the same function that cardboard boxes and plastic crates do today.

For more than 20 years, Dad worked the six-to-two swing shift as a tender at the local paper mill. He'd come home to eat, then head out to his shop. Even though he had already put in eight hours at the mill, his day was really only starting. He'd weave baskets sometimes until nine or ten.

From our beds at night in the summer we could hear him at work. Tap, tap, tap. It was hot, and all the windows were wide open. The only sound was his tap, tap, tap.

One night, Mom yelled out to him, "You're going to keep all the neighbors awake."

Dad called back, "That's right, or the kids will starve."

He made only about $1.60 an hour at the mill—and that wasn't until the 1960s. It took both of Dad's jobs, as well as Mom's at the woolen mill, to keep food on the table for all of us.

We grew up poor, but we didn't know we were poor. We had nothing to compare ourselves to. Everyone in Dresden was poor.

—Ginny Lou Longaberger Wilcox

"We didn't know we were poor"

The J.W. and Bonnie Longaberger dozen: (below; left to right, back) Wendy, Judy, J.W., Bonnie, Genevieve, Jerry, (front) Larry, Dave, Rich, Mary Ann and Ginny Lou; (right) Gary, Carmen and Jeff.

The J.W. Longaberger Collection

A portion of J.W.'s original basket shop.

In 1927, a few years after their initial meeting, J.W. and Bonnie married, and they rented a house adjacent to Guy Ryan's basket factory on Eighth Street. There, they began a family that would eventually comprise six girls and as many boys.

In 1936, during the depths of the Great Depression, the Ryan family sold the basket-making business to J.W. for $1,900; the price included both the factory and the house in which J.W. and Bonnie were living. (Bonnie lives in the same house today, and a portion of the factory still stands out back.) Not long after the purchase, J.W. hung a sign to announce a new name for the enterprise: Ohio Ware Basket Company. For J.W., Bonnie and their children, this home and the

The realization must have triggered a warm rush of panic in the journalist. A reporter for the Zanesville Times Signal *in 1950, he had arrived at the Ohio Ware Basket Company in Dresden to interview a man by the name of Longaberger who handcrafted beautiful baskets.*

The time-honored tradition of the man's family had sounded interesting enough for a full Sunday feature. But as he stood on the cement floor of the small, unpainted shop on Eighth Street, the tall, thin man dressed in work clothes, who went by the initials J.W., responded to all of the questions he asked in short, unquotable sentences.

Of the three boys working alongside their father in the shop that day, the youngest, Rich, hid behind a stack of completed baskets. Another, Larry, like his dad, didn't have a lot to say.

Finally, the eldest boy, Jerry, stepped forward to explain the family's business and basket-making methods. The relieved reporter had a story to write.

"He loved to make baskets"

Now, several decades later, the Sunday feature is an important historical record of J.W.'s reputation as a basket-making master, of his devotion to a family tradition of quality craftsmanship. The few, primitive photographs—the only ones that were ever taken inside the Ohio Ware Basket Company—archive indelibly the portrait of a skilled artisan, the one-time apprentice of his father, passing on the secrets of his trade to his sons.

The enduring image, a cornerstone in the marketing success of Longaberger Baskets, falls short, however, in rendering a true, complete picture of the family. Although Jerry and Larry were the ones most often at their father's side, all six of the oldest Longaberger children put in time in the shop. Having to schedule their hours before and after school and on weekends, they tended at the time to consider the lengthy learning experience as principally one of family duty. None of the children today, however, voices any complaint or regret.

"The way Dad worked wore off on us," says Jerry. "He loved to make baskets and was proud of his craftsmanship. His attitude was to take the time needed to make the best possible basket."

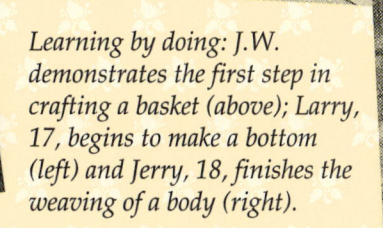

Learning by doing: J.W. demonstrates the first step in crafting a basket (above); Larry, 17, begins to make a bottom (left) and Jerry, 18, finishes the weaving of a body (right).

15

The J.W. Longaberger Collection

basket shop would become the center of their lives.

For the Longabergers—as for most people living in Dresden during the 1930s and 1940s—life was simple but times were hard. They did what they had to do to make ends meet. J.W. took a job at the paper mill, and after laboring there from six in the morning until two in the afternoon, he would come home to share a quick bite to eat with Bonnie, who punched the clock as a spinner on the second shift at the local woolen mill once all the children were in school.

The midday meal rarely lasted more than 15 minutes, then J.W. would unplug his old Philco radio, tuck it under his arm and head out to the basket shop. As the voices of Paul Harvey, Lowell Thomas and assorted soap opera personalities filled the air, J.W. diligently filled orders for baskets.

With 14 people living under the same roof and only a single bathroom, the house on Eighth Street must have been crowded. Funny, though, no one who lived there remembers it that way. A childhood friend of one of the boys, however, recounts that the family was "packed in there like sardines." There were no automatic clothes washers, dishwashers, or microwave ovens, so the housework rarely stopped for Bonnie. Her fondest memories are of raising the children, but she has observed that her moments of greatest happiness were "when all the kids were in their beds."

Naturally, J.W.'s baskets were put to good use in the busy Longaberger home. Bonnie recalls always having laundry baskets to help with the wash of the clothes she made, hamper baskets to keep the bedrooms uncluttered, and gathering baskets for bringing in vegetables from the garden plots out in back of the house. She also

J.W. and Bonnie outside their Eighth Street home, 1942.

made use of several cake baskets and market baskets. And to this day, Bonnie treasures an umbrella basket that J.W. wove for her decades ago.

There were few explicit rules in the Longaberger household, but the children knew that they were expected to be honest and fair, to help each other, and to treat other people the way they wanted to be treated themselves. They had as much freedom as they wanted, as long as they abided by these principles—and as long as they made darn sure that they were home in time for dinner. A tradition of the household, the family always ate the evening meal together.

Out of respect to their parents, the children obeyed and tried not to disappoint. And to make sure that no one got too far out of line, the older

THE J.W. LONGABERGER COLLECTION

Grandma Bonnie at her home in Dresden, the same home in which she and J.W. raised their 12 children.

children kept an eye on the younger ones. As well, J.W. and Bonnie sometimes instinctively knew what the children were up to before they did.

Bonnie is thought by the children to have been generally more lenient than J.W. However, on occasions when rules were broken and guilt was determined beyond a shadow of a doubt, discipline was all but certain. J.W. and Bonnie had as many disciplinary methods as they had children. For example, Dave, the fifth child, was a youngster always on the go. For him, punishment meant having to sit still in a chair. Burdened with this forced inactivity, he usually fell sound asleep.

Jerry, the third child and the oldest boy, tells of a time when he asked his

She prepared meals, did the laundry and cleaned house for a family of 14. She also worked at the local woolen mill.

Yet Bonnie Longaberger put a homemade dessert on the table for dinner every night. Cakes and gingerbread were among the fare that she regularly served. Her pies, offered less often, were an occasion in themselves. Odds were that they would be custard pies (her personal favorite), fresh blackberry pies or her famous apple pies. Odds were better that there were plenty of them. There was no question that they were good.

When Bonnie baked pies, she did five, six, maybe seven at a time. Knowing the appetite of her family, she cut generous portions—nothing smaller than a quarter of a pie. Leftovers, her motive in making so many pies at once, were rare.

"When did she find the time?"

GRANDMA BONNIE'S APPLE PIES

—Editor's Note: To prepare just one of Grandma Bonnie's Apple Pies, simply cut by half the ingredients listed.

PIE CRUST
4 cups flour
1 tablespoon sugar
1-1/2 teaspoons salt
1-1/2 cups lard
1 egg (beaten)
1 tablespoon vinegar
1/2 cup water
(Makes two double-crust or lattice-top pies)

Sift together flour, sugar and salt in a large bowl. With a pastry blender or two knives, cut in lard until mixture resembles course crumbs. Mix together egg, vinegar and water. Add wet ingredients to dry ingredients and mix until dough is moist enough to hold together when formed into a ball. Wrap dough in plastic wrap and refrigerate until well chilled—at least 30 minutes.

Roll dough on a lightly-floured surface. Cut two 12-inch circles of dough and place each one in a Grandma Bonnie's Apple Pie Plate. Crimp edges of dough to form a decorative rim and prick bottom repeatedly with a fork. Set crusts in freezer until pie filling has been prepared.

PIE FILLING
6 cups apples (pared, cored and sliced)
1 teaspoon cinnamon
2 cups sugar
4 tablespoons butter or margarine
6 teaspoons flour
6 tablespoons milk
(Makes filling for two pies)

Preheat oven to 375 degrees. Stirring gently, mix together apples, flour, sugar and spices. Place mixture on frozen pie crusts, then dab on butter or margarine and pour milk over top. Place top crusts or lattice strips. Bake for 40 to 45 minutes.

The J.W. Longaberger Collection

father for a quarter so he could go to a movie with a friend. J.W. turned him down and Jerry accepted the answer, informing his friend that he couldn't go. The friend urged Jerry to press the matter further, but the Longaberger boy knew better. Jerry figured his dad would count up the times he had to say "no" and apply all the extras to future requests. "That's the way my dad was," notes Rich, the sixth child. "When he said 'no,' he meant 'no.'"

The Longaberger family struggled at times and had to pull together to make ends meet. Like most of the families in Dresden, they went without a lot of things. Once J.W. was married, he never owned a car until the early 1960s, when he bought a pickup truck. The children didn't have bikes, roller skates or fancy new clothes. To come by such an item, they bought it themselves with money they had earned. Despite the struggles, Bonnie stretched food as far as it would go, even on the occasions when one of the children came home with an unexpected guest for dinner. The only extravagance that the children remember was a television set; one of the first in Dresden, it made them, for a time, the envy of the neighborhood.

Moments of high excitement came every so often when a truck would stop by to haul away a shipment of J.W.'s pottery ware baskets. There would be much strutting about by the Longaberger children when the youngsters from the neighborhood turned up to see what the commotion was about. A little less noticeable, but just as important to the family's well-being, were the regular knocks at the door as people came by to order baskets. Sometimes J.W. would have what was needed on hand, but often he was asked to custom-make a basket for a particular task.

J.W.'s legacy lives on in today's basket-making process

J.W.'s approach to his craft was passed to his children, and from them to their children and an extended family of many thousands of weavers who are now employed by the Company. But while the scale of basket-making operations has changed considerably, the methods haven't. Today's time-honored techniques for handmade baskets are presented in the following photo essay.

J.W. selected the finest hardwood

In a ritual that took place a couple of times each year, J.W. walked Copeland's Woods outside Dresden, selecting trees of the finest hardwood to be made into his weaving materials. J.W. usually wove pottery ware baskets from splints of hickory, but he used maple for such items as his market and cake baskets. Carrying a two-man crosscut saw, Larry and Jerry accompanied their dad on the eight-mile hike to the woods. Genevieve, the oldest child, often went, too, her own saw in hand.

There was little talk as J.W. conducted his search. He usually could tell by sight if a tree was suitable; any suspicion of it being past maturity and starting to decay was settled by a knock. An acceptable tree had to offer at least two 10- to 12-foot lengths of solid timber, free of knots and other imperfections.

Taking turns on one end of the saw, Larry and Jerry would help J.W. cut as many as 20 trees. Once felled, the trees were cut into logs and dragged out of the woods by a team of horses. The logs were loaded onto a truck and driven 80 miles to Marietta, Ohio, to be shaved into veneer sheets and clipped into weaving materials. Since he took only mature trees, helping a stand of timber by giving the younger trees room to grow, J.W. never had to pay for his logs. He only had to clean up the woods when he was done. (Selective harvesting, as this practice is now called, is required of Longaberger's log suppliers today.)

J.W. was known to dye splints for accents. Blue was a color he liked. He would soak the splints in a vat of clothing dye and hot water until they were a shade that pleased him.

Stacks of hardwood veneer are clipped into weaving materials, the dimensions of which are carefully checked.

Splints to be used as color accents in baskets are soaked in vats containing a solution of dye and warm water (right). Sorted color-accent splints (below) are kept cool to resist mold.

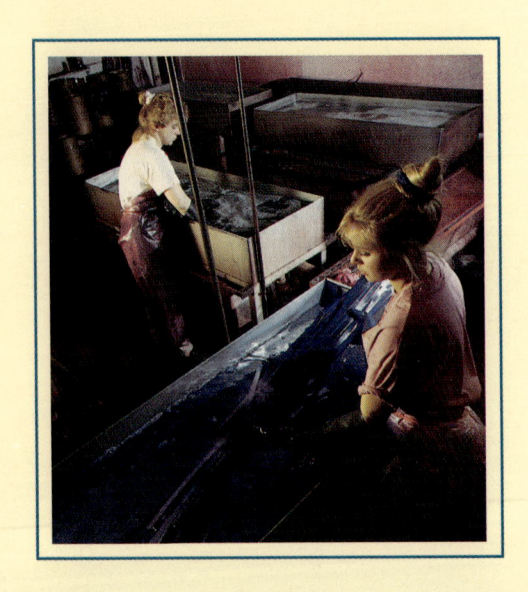

The Company's dye team at the Hartville facility.

A craftsman who builds the wooden form for a basket (below) has an exacting task. The form serves as a mold and is used repeatedly. It must be precisely crafted (right) to ensure that the baskets are the right shape and size.

27

A bottom is literally the foundation of a basket, and its splints must be spaced uniformly (above). Completed bottoms (right) are sent on to weavers.

29

J.W. wove baskets to last generations

Selecting trees for J.W.'s weaving materials was not a scientific process, and splints sometimes returned from Marietta riddled with knots, or in some other way ill-suited for weaving. Bonnie recalls knowing if splints were good simply by the look on J.W.'s face: "He had these dark brown eyes and you could always tell when he was out of sorts."

J.W. always dried his splints carefully. One reason was to prevent mildew: He would never take money for a basket with mildew. Another reason was that he took pride in the tight weave of his baskets, which added to their strength and durability. One way he got a tight weave was by drying splints as soon as possible, thereby "pre-shrinking" them.

Dried splints were kept on racks in a back room of the shop. To make dried splints pliable again for weaving, J.W. would soak them in water, then wrap them in a sheet of felt and store them overnight. The woven baskets were dried outside in the sun or, in cold weather, hung from the ceiling of the heated shop. Since most of the shrinkage had already occurred, the baskets held their shape.

J.W. made a round, inverted bottom by weaving splints around upsplints laid out in a pattern resembling an asterisk. A flat, rectangular bottom was made using a form. With a completed bottom secured to a basket form, J.W. would proceed to weave the body of the basket, running horizontal rows over and under the upsplints and stopping to tap the weave tight. With the body fully woven, he trimmed the upsplints and tacked on two bands at the top, one inside and one outside.

With the form placed on a weaving horse,
a basket bottom is carefully positioned and
secured with a screw-down.

*A woven, round, inverted bottom
is constructed around a wooden form.*

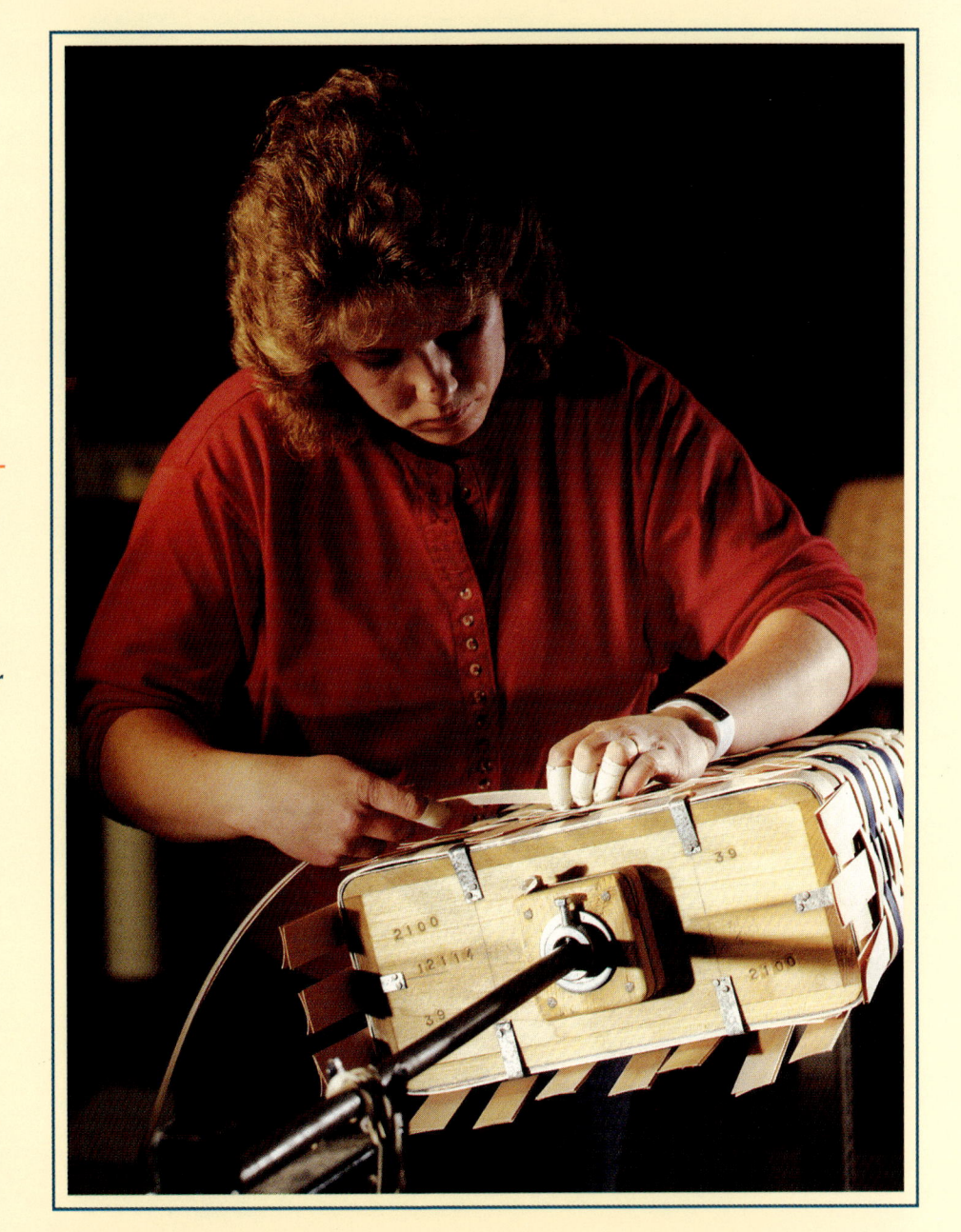

The basket takes shape as successive rows are alternately woven over and under the upsplints.

A tool called a tapper cushions the force of a hammer as the weaver tightens the rows.

Once the basket is fully woven, the weaver trims the surplus off the upsplints—a procedure known as "giving the basket a haircut."

At evenly spaced intervals, tacks are driven through the center of the trim strip and top band to secure them to the upsplints.

*Gently striking a tapper with
a hammer, the weaver eases the
basket off the form.*

*The weaver smooths any rough
spots along the basket's
rim using fine sandpaper.*

*Dating and initialing of the fully woven
basket by the weaver tell of the
pride of personal craftsmanship and
attention to quality.*

Every handcrafted basket is closely inspected against a lengthy, detailed list of criteria by Longaberger's experienced quality assurance personnel.

J.W.'s baskets were made to order

When a customer came by to purchase a basket, J.W. would discuss options such as handles and lids. He carved handles by hand, choosing oak because he could split suitable pieces from a block of the wood with relative ease. J.W. would shave a handle down smooth, tapering the ends to fit snugly between the tight weaves of the basket without altering its shape.

He placed handles in a trough of water to make them pliable, and molded them into shape around a curved handle form. The handle of a basket made by J.W. has a distinctive feel, worn smooth from use, but still slightly wavy to the touch.

J.W. attached his handles with tacks driven through the top bands, catching the tops of two upsplints. A trademark habit was to drive the three tacks that secured the handle ends in a triangular pattern.

J.W. seldom made baskets with swinging handles; those few were usually his picnic baskets. To attach swinging handles, he drilled holes through the top bands and through the ends of the handle pieces. He then aligned the holes and fastened them with metal rivets. Today, wooden washers and copper rivets are used.

Hardwood lids also were attached to some baskets with pieces of leather as the hinges. J.W. would tack the leather pieces onto the rim at the rear of the basket and then tack through them into the lid. He installed rawhide loops and wood knobs for fastening the lids in a closed position. These methods are still in use today.

Hardwood strips are cut to length for stationary and swinging handles (left), then soaked in hot water to prepare them for shaping. Molded into curves around forms, the handles are stacked in the drying room (below) until they are ready for sanding.

41

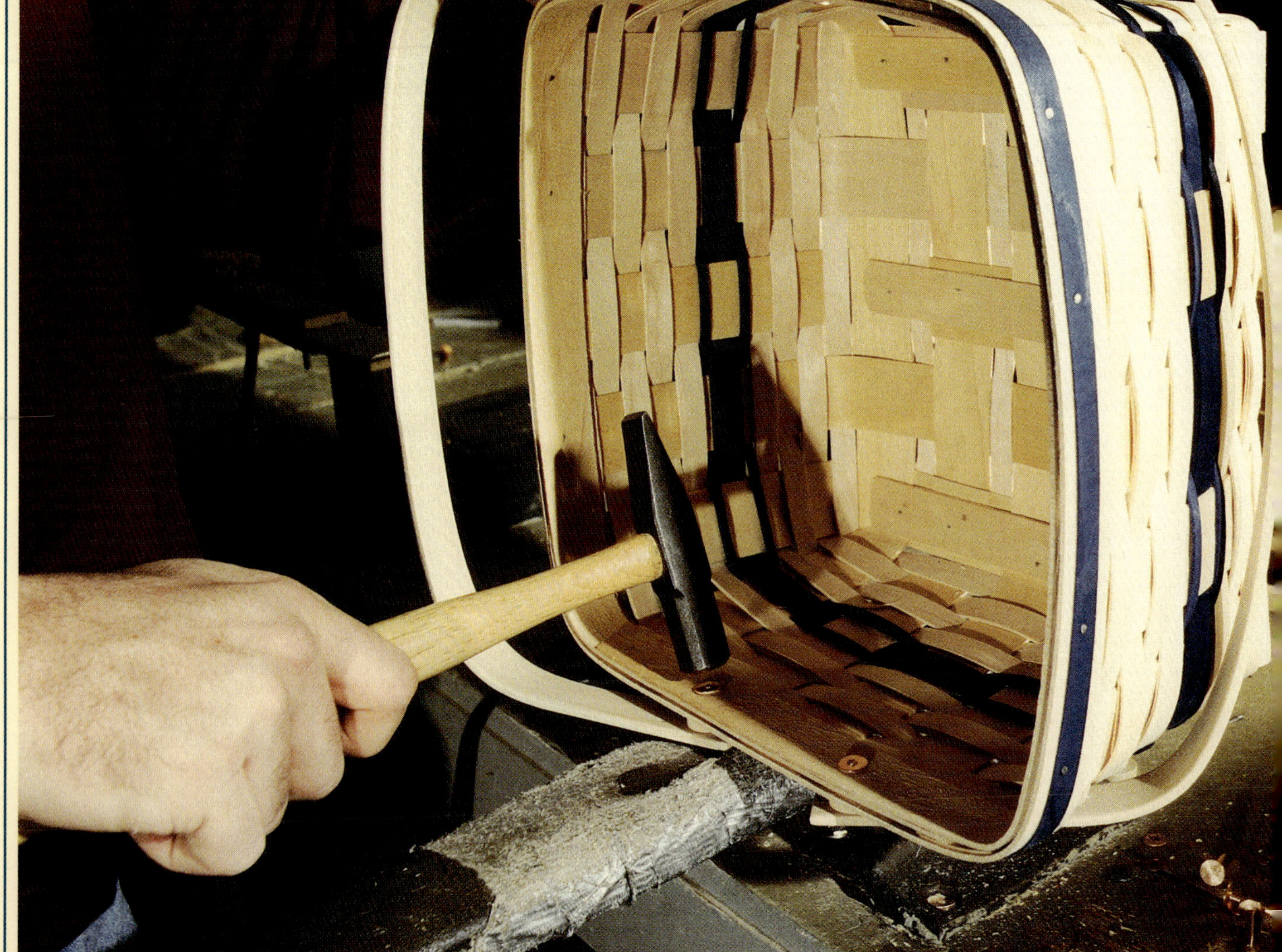

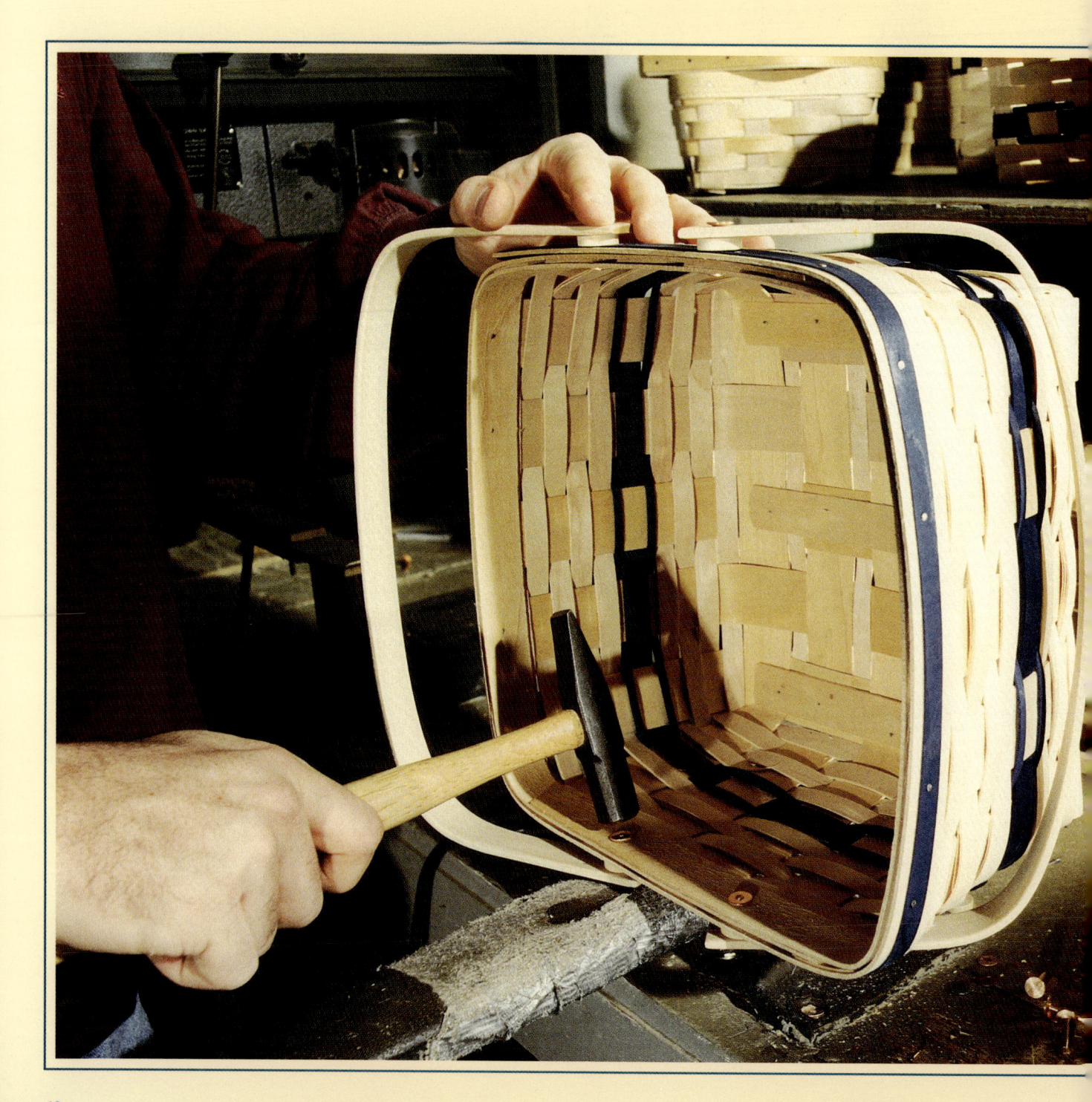

Each end of a swinging handle is installed using a wooden washer and copper rivet (left). A stationary handle is fitted into place (above), then secured with tacks.

The weaver tacks the ends of a leather strip in place (left). A second strip fastened the same way (right) completes the handle on one side of a Corn Basket.

45

Each basket of the J.W. Longaberger Collection features a commemorative brass tag on the trim strip.

*After the basket has passed
through the staining chamber,
excess stain is wiped off
with a cloth.*

*The same care that goes
into the making of baskets is
exercised in the shipping
department, where each
basket is individually
wrapped in tissue paper and
boxed for the journey
to the customer's home.*

49

Inheriting a legacy

Over the years, J.W. produced many thousands of pottery ware baskets for various companies. The number of baskets he made for use in homes and farms was, by comparison, relatively small. But these latter baskets are the ones for which J.W. is best known. People came from miles around to buy the baskets J.W. created for carrying groceries home from the market, taking baked goods to social gatherings, feeding livestock, going on picnics, doing the wash and bringing in food from the garden.

As Rich explains, "Dad made baskets of every conceivable geometric shape. If you wanted to buy a basket from us, you came to the door and asked for it. We had a bit of an inventory in a corner of the shop. Other than that, they were special orders."

Completely dedicated to his craft, J.W. took it as his mission to make the strongest, most durable baskets possi-

---

Made to last, J.W.'s baskets still turn up in unlikely places. The hunt for one of the baskets he made can be worth the effort. An original worth thousands of dollars on the collector's market may go unnoticed for a few dollars at a garage sale.

Ginny Lou paid $1,000 for a pottery ware basket that her father made out of rattan in the late 1920s. The woman who sold the original was happy; unaware of its value, she had been seeking five dollars for it. And Ginny Lou is delighted to have the basket back in her family.

Antique shops, flea markets and garage sales in the area of Dresden and nearby Zanesville are the most fertile ground for discovery of a basket made by J.W. But identifying one can be difficult. J.W. never signed his baskets, and his shop was one of several making baskets in the area in his time.

Fortunately for collectors, there are a few trademark characteristics by which a J.W. original usually may be distinguished:

THE J.W. LONGABERGER COLLECTION

Identifying the master's originals

J.W. trademarks: a stamped label (above, left), a triangular pattern of tacks at the handle (above, right), braiding along the rim and a carved oak handle (above).

Stamped label: "Ohio Ware Basket Company" and "Made in Dresden, Ohio" were two stamps J.W. used on occasion to label his baskets.
Tack pattern: J.W. fastened stationary handles with three, triangularly placed tacks often a size smaller than others used on the baskets.
Handle thickness: Baskets made by J.W. until the 1950s featured hand-carved handles of varying thickness; later handles were saw-cut.
Braiding: Cake baskets and clothes hampers were among creations that J.W. often trimmed with a fine-twine braid on the rim or handle.
Colors: J.W. was fond of using dyed accents, especially as Easter approached. His "Dresden blue" is a hallmark of the J.W. Collection.
Bottom style: The bottoms of J.W.'s early rectangular-shaped baskets featured an open weave with sizeable gaps. Only in the 1950s did he begin to make baskets using the style of closed bottoms with which today's Longaberger enthusiasts have become familiar.

51

The J.W. Longaberger Collection

Rich Longaberger, now Assistant to the Chief Operating Officer, on the weaving floor at the Longaberger factory.

ble—even if that meant his customers didn't have to buy so many of them. For example, his early pottery ware baskets featured two upside-down U-shaped stationary handles on opposite sides of the rim. Workers in the mills would tie ropes to the handles and drag the baskets when they were heavy with a load of pottery. This took its toll and the handles would eventually snap, so J.W. fashioned sturdier handles cut out of the sides of the baskets under the rim. To a pure

*W*hen J.W. opened his newly-aquired shop in the 1930s, the vast majority of the baskets he crafted were destined for Ohio's pottery mills. Cardboard boxes were then not in widespread use, and the pottery mills used baskets to transport materials from station to station. The large, round baskets that J.W. made for this purpose were reinforced with steel bands. For a dozen of his creations, he received the sum of $12.50.

As the Company's horizons broadened into the 1990s, pottery was consequently a natural first choice for diversification of the product line. Within a year of the launching of Longaberger Pottery, which at the time was limited to two pitchers, three mixing bowls, Grandma Bonnie's Apple Pie Plate and the Bread Basket Warming

Renewing a link with tradition

Brick, demand was outpacing the production capacity of the pottery mill used by the Company in Roseville, Ohio.

In 1991 pottery production was moved to the Hall China Company and the Sterling China Company in East Liverpool, Ohio—two mills where J.W. had once shipped many of his pottery ware baskets. The pottery line also has been greatly expanded, and now includes five-piece sets of dinnerware, serving platters and bowls, salt and pepper shakers, mugs, creamers and sugar bowls. Each piece is produced following the Longaberger design entitled Woven Traditions™, which features color-accented, in-relief strips of weave on an ivory background; there is now a choice of color accent, Classic Blue, the first offered, or Heritage Green.

Just like the baskets of the J.W. Longaberger Collection, pieces of Longaberger Pottery have become valuable collectibles. Especially collectible are the early pieces that were produced in Roseville and special pieces made in Traditional Red, of which availability was limited. Also much sought after are the Santa Cookie Molds of the 1990 to 1993 series, precursor to the four-year series of Angel Cookie Molds that began in 1993.

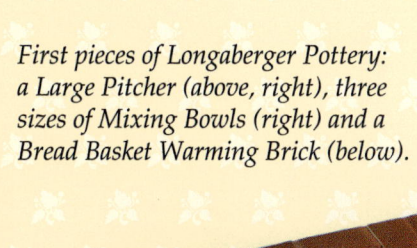

First pieces of Longaberger Pottery: a Large Pitcher (above, right), three sizes of Mixing Bowls (right) and a Bread Basket Warming Brick (below).

The J.W. Longaberger Collection

Gary Longaberger, Director of Longaberger WoodCrafts™.

craftsman, the modification made sense since the baskets were stronger and more durable. But since the mills needed fewer replacement baskets, the change also meant a loss of sales. When someone pointed this out, J.W. is said to have replied dryly: "That's not the idea."

J.W.'s philosophy on his craft was passed to his children as they began to learn the trade. Although Genevieve, first of the Longaberger brood, was also first to work in the shop, Jerry and Larry, the eldest sons, became mainstays in the business and went through a lengthy apprenticeship. Dave and Rich worked there later as well. Ultimately, they were able to complete entire baskets to J.W.'s exacting standards. True to his nature, J.W. didn't give a lot of verbal instructions. He believed that his children would learn best by doing.

When people approached J.W. with special needs in a basket, he always did his best to accommodate them. And he certainly had an extraordinary knack for finding solutions to problems. In fact, that's how many of the baskets in the J.W. Collection came into existence.

For example, as automobiles grew in popularity during the 1930s and '40s, J.W. came up with a new basket that would still be convenient for carrying into the market yet fit neatly between the bucket seats of a car. He achieved this end simply, but ingeniously, by cutting in half lengthwise the form for his larger market basket. His "automobile basket," later called the Bread and Milk Basket, finds new life today as the Magazine Basket.

Jerry (left) and Larry, with one of their father's original forms and a weaving horse dating back to the 1920s.

55

THE J.W. LONGABERGER COLLECTION

Such household baskets were near and dear to J.W.'s heart, but throughout the 1930s and '40s, at least 80 percent of his business was in providing pottery ware baskets. When he was able to sell these products directly to his customers he got a pretty good price, sometimes as much as $32.50 for a dozen. But as a wholesaler, he received only $12.50 per dozen and even with typical orders of ten dozen baskets, demand simply wasn't great enough to sustain the business indefinitely. As the years passed, the Ohio potteries began to lock up their doors and J.W.'s orders declined. By the early 1950s, they had ceased altogether.

As the Ohio Ware Basket Company hung on by a thread in 1951, Jerry, then in his early twenties, took a job away from home and made baskets only part-time, leaving Larry to work full-time in the shop with his father. Things got worse for the business the following year, and both Jerry and Larry took factory jobs in nearby Newark, Ohio. It was the end of an

Two of the lucky ones

During J.W.'s lifetime, his baskets were always such common sights in Dresden that no one paid them much notice. Today, the opposite is true: Coming across a J.W. original is a rare occurrence that attracts everyone's attention.

56

Mary E. Hahn recalls the familiarity of J.W.'s original banker's waste baskets at Dresden's First Trust and Savings Bank when she began working there in 1951. She is proud to still have on the job with her one of the round, braid-trimmed baskets that all survived a move and several name changes of the bank. Mary also owns a number of other J.W. originals, including a market basket she inherited from her mother and an Easter basket she received as a gift from her parents.

When Max Hittle needed a couple of tough, durable corn baskets to use on his farm in 1958, he went directly to J.W.: the supplier his parents had always relied on, and the helpful handyman who, along with son Gary, would assist in the building of his brick farmhouse in the early 1960s. One of the baskets that Max bought endured more than ten years of punishing work in the fields before being run over by a tractor. The other basket, having withstood several additional decades of use, is still intact albeit somewhat misshapen—Max describes it as "whopper-jawed"—and has been retired to a comfortable spot in the family living room. There is only one detail about the baskets that Max, 36 years after his purchase, has trouble recollecting. "I'm not sure what I paid for them. Maybe five or six dollars." No matter what their exact cost was, though, he considers the money to have been extremely well spent.

Mary E. Hahn holds her original banker's waste basket at the bank where she works (above, left). Max Hittle, a schoolmate of Dave's, sits to the right of one of his original corn baskets in the basement of his farmhouse (above).

57

The J.W. Longaberger Collection

era. J.W. continued to weave nearly every day until the late 1950s, but he was mainly producing market baskets and sales were never sensational. In 1959, the Dresden paper mill closed its doors and for the first time in his life, J.W. found himself without a job.

During the 1960s, as the middle and younger children began leaving home, J.W. took a series of jobs. He worked for a time as a finishing carpenter with his tenth child, Gary, who had become a gifted woodworker. Later, J.W. worked on farms in rural Ohio building chicken coops—a job he wound up hating because of his keen aversion to travel. He continued to weave baskets throughout these years, by then mostly as a pastime or upon special request.

Two of the baskets that J.W. made during this period were commissioned by a neighbor, Josephine Lindsey. Josephine asked J.W. to weave baskets she could use for carrying coal and wood to the fireplace. For the coal basket, J.W. used the body

Often working alone in his rudimentary shop at the back of the family home, J.W. filled orders for thousands of baskets while listening to the radio. To accommodate the thousands of weavers who today fill orders for millions of baskets, the Company uses all one million square feet of its Dresden factory, where music videos are broadcast on a closed-circuit television network.

Other than the scale of activity, however, there is remarkably little

A married couple who are weavers on one of the Company's work teams.

A business still defined by family

difference between the two workplace settings. Baskets are still crafted entirely by hand, following the same time-honored methods that J.W. passed on to his children. And the rigorous standards of quality that J.W. observed are applied just as diligently today.

Another striking similarity in the two workplace settings is the prevalence of family. Just as J.W. brought his children into his shop, the Company welcomes all kinds of family combinations on its workforce—from husbands and wives and fathers and daughters to aunts and nieces and cousins and in-laws. Family members are a part of the makeup of every department throughout the Company; often, members of the same family work side by side.

Weavers on one of the Company's work teams: a bride-to-be (left) with her fiancé (seated) and his parents.

In part, this characteristic of the Company is the natural result of a labor-intensive business operating in a rural area with a relatively small population from which to draw employees. But the Company views its family environment as a great strength—one that breeds unity in the pursuit of common goals.

By keeping a close eye on the past, the Company has moved ahead in ways compatible with its origins. Technology is applied when it makes sense, but never simply to eliminate a hands-on procedure. And the grouping of workers into teams keeps alive the vibrant spirit of a small shop in what is now the world's largest basket-making factory.

As its business horizons continue to grow, one of the Company's objectives is to preserve the atmosphere of a small, family shop while rewarding employees with the benefits of a large corporation. At Longaberger, the more things may change, the more they seem to become the same.

The J.W. Longaberger Collection

form of a picnic basket and lined it with particle board. The lining fit the finished basket so perfectly that Josephine never had to worry about scattering coal dust. The wood basket was equally impressive: J.W. gave it a special handle that circled the bottom for added strength. Both baskets were used regularly up until 1983. (Mrs. Lindsey later donated the coal basket to the Longaberger Museum.) Even if he was now designing and crafting baskets only as a hobby, J.W. clearly hadn't lost his touch.

With J.W. in his sixties, grandchildren became a big part of the scene. This was especially true during the annual Longaberger reunion, held each summer at the Eighth Street house. It was during these gatherings that the grandchildren formed their lasting memories of Grandpa Longaberger. Recalls Tami, Dave's first daughter: "Longaberger family reunions were *large* reunions. There were children everywhere—and lots of baskets. Grandpa Longaberger was always there. What I remember most about him was that he was the quiet patriarch. He was quiet, but clearly in charge. He didn't have to say much to get his point across. A glance either way would do the job." J.W. tended to be far more lenient with his grandchildren than he ever was with their parents. He even let the little ones play in the basket shop, which he had always frowned upon in earlier years.

In 1972, about the time J.W. turned seventy, his son Dave came forward with a business proposition. Dave asked his father to weave a few dozen baskets that he would try to sell in his grocery store in Dresden and distribute to other stores in the area. Dave wanted to bring the family's basket-making heritage back.

Considering that Dave had actively tried to escape working in the shop through most of his youth, J.W. may have found the idea farfetched. But he also knew that Dave was not an idler, having always been down on Main

Dave in the '80s, installing the handle on a market basket for a promotional photograph.

Street hustling work in one business or another and earning one of his nicknames: the 25-cent millionaire.

Dave explained his plan this way: He had noticed an increase in the number of wicker baskets turning up in retail stores as home decorator items. He knew firsthand that J.W.'s baskets were superior in quality to those he was seeing. He also knew that his dad still loved to make baskets—that he needed to pursue his craft. J.W. went along with the plan and Dave christened the venture J.W.'s Handwoven Baskets. Typically optimistic, Dave was encouraged by the initial uneven sales of the baskets.

Sadly, his father would not live to see the business prosper. Master craftsman J.W. Longaberger died of a heart attack on April 10, 1973. He was seventy-one years old.

In the weeks that followed, Dave decided to carry on with the venture in spite of J.W.'s death. Larry agreed to help train a handful of weavers in their father's methods and get them started making baskets.

For his part, Dave played the role of entrepreneur. Following his business instincts, he became intrigued by a dilapidated building that had once housed the woolen mill where his mother had worked. Despite the age and run-down appearance of the building, Dave envisioned it equipped with rows of weaving horses and filled with the buzz of basket makers at work. Dave agreed to buy the building for $7,000; he would pay

The J.W. Longaberger Collection

$200 a month. The decision brought his vision one step closer to reality. Twenty years later, the $7,000 building would be corporate headquarters to a multimillion-dollar basket business.

Within a few months, Dave had the building in tolerable condition and a handful of weavers were hard at work, making baskets while chatting and listening to the radio. His desire to carry on the family's heritage was fulfilled. Dave's business began to experience moderate success, but nothing approaching the level he was hoping for. He knew the baskets could be popular, if only people knew the history about them. The legacy that the baskets represented just wasn't getting across to customers in a retail setting. Not to most customers, that is.

Charleen Cuckovich was an admirer of baskets long before the eventful day in 1977 when, acting on curiosity, she arrived at Dave's fledgling enterprise and, acting on a hunch, ended up driving off with $200

Although J.W. never signed his baskets, initialing and dating of completed baskets has evolved into an expression of pride and craftsmanship cherished by Longaberger Basket collectors. And like so many meaningful acts, the practice wasn't decided upon in a stuffy boardroom. It just happened.

Stopping at a small shop in Walnut Creek, Ohio, Charleen Cuckovich was captivated by a simple display of 15 baskets. A collector of antiques and handmade crafts, she'd never before seen baskets of such character and quality; and antique baskets of comparable beauty were never as reasonably priced. She bought the baskets and learned from the shop owner that they were made by a family named Longaberger in nearby Dresden. Her husband was persuaded to make the town their next stop.

They weren't disappointed when about two hours later they arrived in Dresden. At the north end of Chestnut Street, they found

"An expression of pride by the craftsman"

Charleen Cuckovich, Longaberger's first Consultant and now a Sales Director.

the basket factory, a run-down building almost hidden by bushes and weeds. Undaunted, they went in. Almost five hours passed before they came out.

Charleen was spellbound. She was curious about all the baskets that hung on the walls. She asked about the Longaberger family and the history of the baskets. She was fascinated by a weaver who was crafting a gathering basket on the lone horse at the center of the floor.

Remembering the signatures she'd noticed on the bottom of the expensive antique baskets she so admired, Charleen asked the weaver to sign the completed basket. The weaver signed it: "Made by Bonnie Hague, Aug. 22, 1977." Thus was born a new tradition.

The inscription practice was integrated into Charleen's sales approach for Longaberger Baskets. "It was part of the way I sold baskets," she says, now a Sales Director for the Company. "It personalizes them and identifies them as handmade. People recognize and appreciate it as an expression of pride by the craftsman."

63

THE J.W. LONGABERGER COLLECTION

worth of baskets. Back home in Lordstown, she proceeded to sell the baskets to her friends and relatives at home shows, becoming the first Sales Consultant. More important, Dave realized that this new method of selling would allow the story of the baskets to be communicated. The new marketing relationship between Dave and Charleen was going to help put J.W.'s baskets in millions of homes across the country.

Of her early association with the Company, Charleen recalls, "Dave needed someone like me and I needed someone like him. He believed I could sell his baskets and I believed he could make them. Those first six months I sold thousands of baskets. From the very beginning I knew everybody wanted them."

As the frequency of home shows increased, Dave shared the workload and the Company refined its marketing story based on the Longaberger family history. On any night of the week, groups of women were gather-

"Creating opportunities for success"

Longaberger women have always played active roles in the family. No less powerful is their influence in the basket-making legacy that is now in the hands of a fourth generation.

A working-mother pioneer, J.W.'s wife, Bonnie, took a job as a spinner at the local woolen mill to help support the family once all 12 children were in school. Genevieve, by right of being the eldest child, was first to help in J.W.'s shop. Second in line, Wendy periodically rode around selling J.W.'s baskets door-to-door with Grandpa Dave, Bonnie's father.

Today, J.W.'s son Dave guides the Company's helm with the help of his own two daughters: Tami Longaberger Kaido and Rachel Longaberger Schmidt. Tami, now

Rachel (left) and Tami at the home office in Dresden.

"Tami and Rachel know the way I want things done," says proud father Dave. "They've been here since day one and seen the method to the madness."

Tami and Rachel agree on the lessons they've learned. Says Tami, "Dad has taught us that success is the reward of hard work. We've seen him work hard every day for 30 years; he has never slowed down for even a minute."

Rachel adds, "Creating opportunities for success, not just for the family, but for all of our employees and sales field as well, is one of the biggest strengths that Dad has given to the Company. And we have also learned from Dad the importance of having fun and enjoying our work—because life is too short."

President, began her career in the basket-making business as a tour guide at the factory. Rachel made product tags before she went on to Employee Communications, from where she was promoted to Director of Human Resources; she is now Chief Operating Officer.

65

THE J.W. LONGABERGER COLLECTION

The history and heritage of Longaberger Baskets come alive during home shows conducted by Sales Associates.

ing in Ohio living rooms to socialize and to hear about J.W. Longaberger, the care and pride he wove into his hardwood baskets. Dresden, Bonnie, Dave and the rest of the family came to life for the listeners, stepping them back to simpler times when baskets were a part of daily life. As baskets passed from hand to hand, the quality, tradition and years of dedication that went into them could be felt.

Word of the baskets spread quickly throughout Ohio, and orders began to trickle in from neighboring Indiana and Pennsylvania. Dave was starting to see what he believed would happen all along. Continued growth of the business into the early 1980s brought the realization that women were key to the Company's success. "Women are very intuitive," notes Tami, who accompanied her father to many of his home shows. "They want to know the story behind the product. There is no question that if it weren't for women and their perspective on these products, we wouldn't be here. If it weren't for them expressing an interest in our family and J.W., there wouldn't be a J.W. Longaberger Collection."

The J.W. Longaberger Collection

The baskets for which J.W. is most remembered were crafted with an eye to the specific needs of his family, neighbors and friends. Twelve of these very special baskets were selected for the J.W. Longaberger Collection and are presented in the pages that follow, along with their stories and photographs of the originals on which they are based.

1 9 8 3

MARKET
BASKET

For the households of J.W.'s time, a trip to the market on Main Street was a daily necessity. Because there was no refrigeration, goods that could spoil had to be purchased as needed and used right away. Always alert to specific, chore-related tasks, the practical-minded J.W. created a market basket especially suited to this fact of life for Dresden's townsfolk. His original design inspired the J.W. Market Basket, the Collection's first edition, of which more than 6,000 were sold.

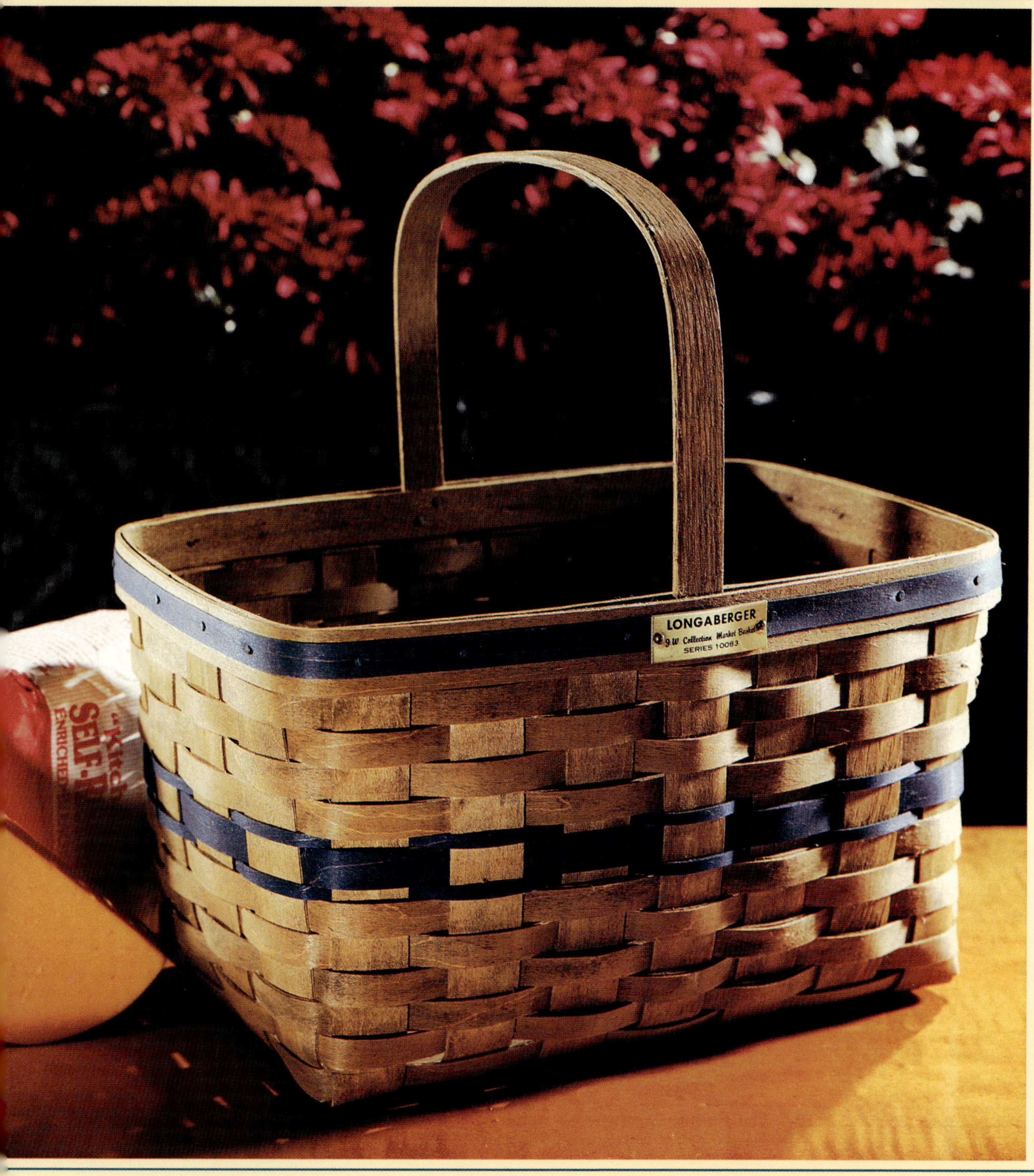
LONGABERGER
J.W. Collection Market Basket
SERIES 10083

1 9 8 4

WASTE BASKET

*A*n orange crate from the local grocery store was used by J.W. as the form for his waste baskets—not surprising, given his reputation for practical mindedness. J.W. wanted a waste basket that was tough and at the same time attractive enough to be on display. His original waste basket was as finely crafted as it was useful. Even today, some of the waste baskets J.W. made are in use in Dresden businesses. The J.W. Waste Basket was offered as the Collection's second edition, and approximately 3,500 were sold.

LONGABERGER
J.W. Collection Waste Basket
SERIES 20084

1 9 8 5

Apple
Basket

In the 1930s, a local orchard owner came to J.W. with a problem: How could he keep his apples from rotting before they were sent off to market? Knowing that the inverted bottoms of his pottery baskets allowed for ample air circulation, J.W. incorporated a similarly shaped woven bottom into his apple basket, which also featured a gentle, upward taper. J.W.'s elegantly functional design was reintroduced as the third edition of the Collection, and approximately 10,500 J.W. Apple Baskets were purchased.

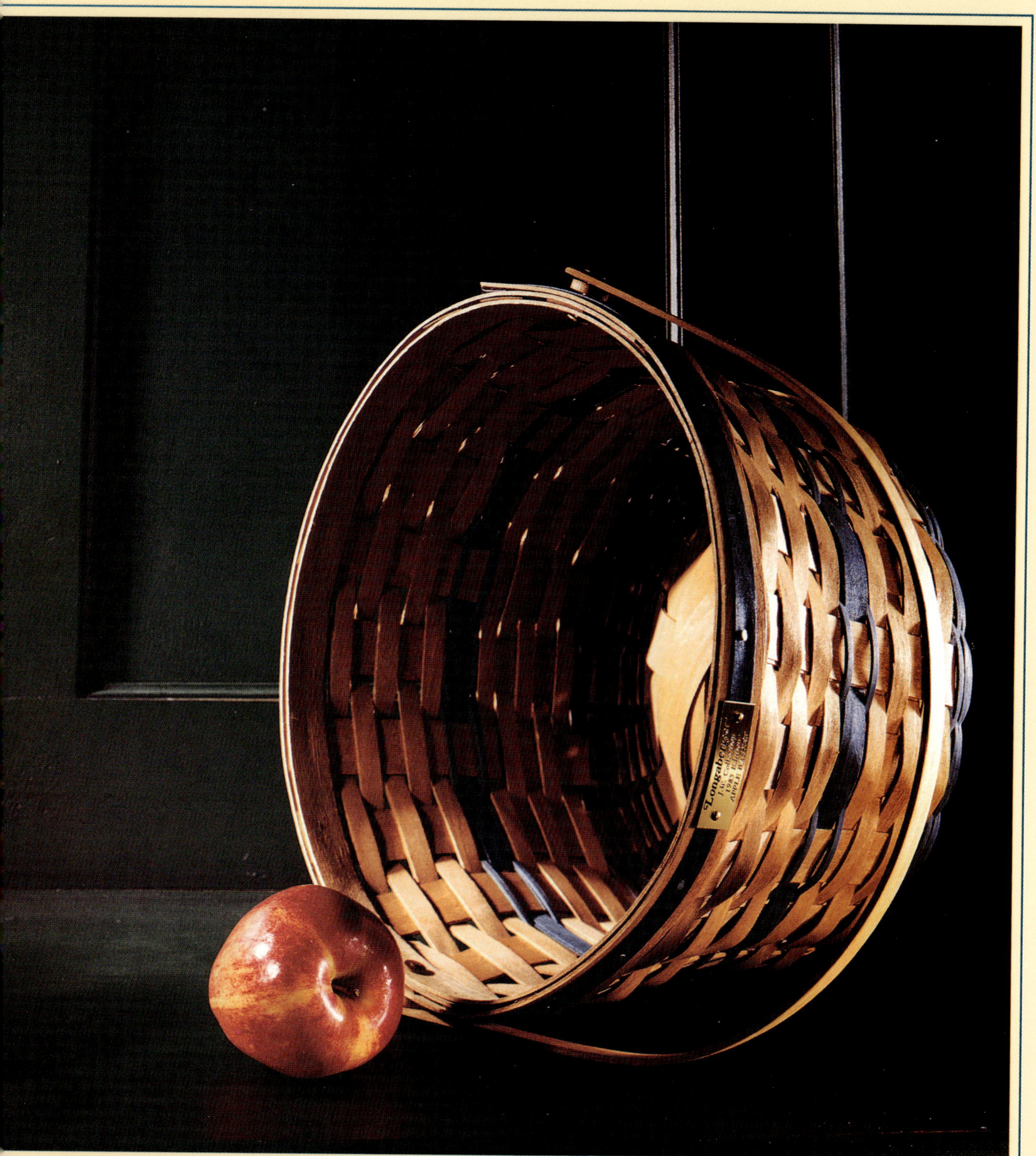

1 9 8 6

TWO-PIE BASKET

One pie was never enough for any thoughtful baker to bring to a church social. And so the folks of Dresden would have less trouble carrying their pies, J.W. designed the two-pie basket. With the first pie resting on the bottom of the basket, a wood divider resembling a small, square table was placed in the basket with the second pie placed on top of that. J.W.'s two-pie basket was a welcomed sight around town. Approximately 44,000 of the Collection's fourth edition were sold.

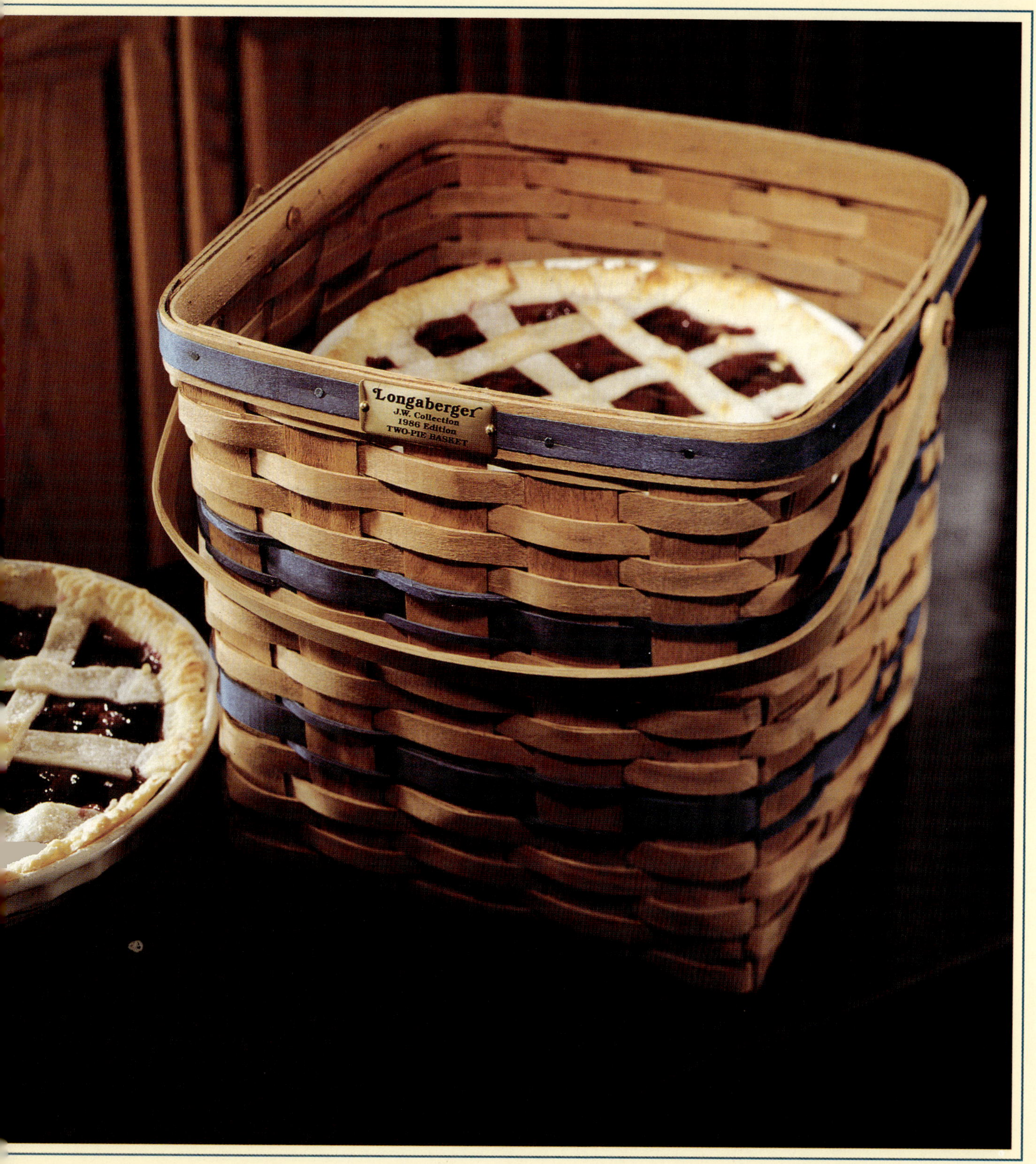
Longaberger
J.W. Collection
1986 Edition
TWO-PIE BASKET

1 9 8 7

BREAD AND MILK
BASKET

*B*y cutting the form for a market basket in half, J.W. created the bread and milk basket, referred to during his era as the automobile basket, since he designed it to fit between the two front bucket seats. J.W.'s originals quickly became popular in Dresden for quick jaunts to the market for the day's basic food staples. The J.W. Bread and Milk Basket was issued as the fifth edition of the Collection, and approximately 18,000 of them were sold.

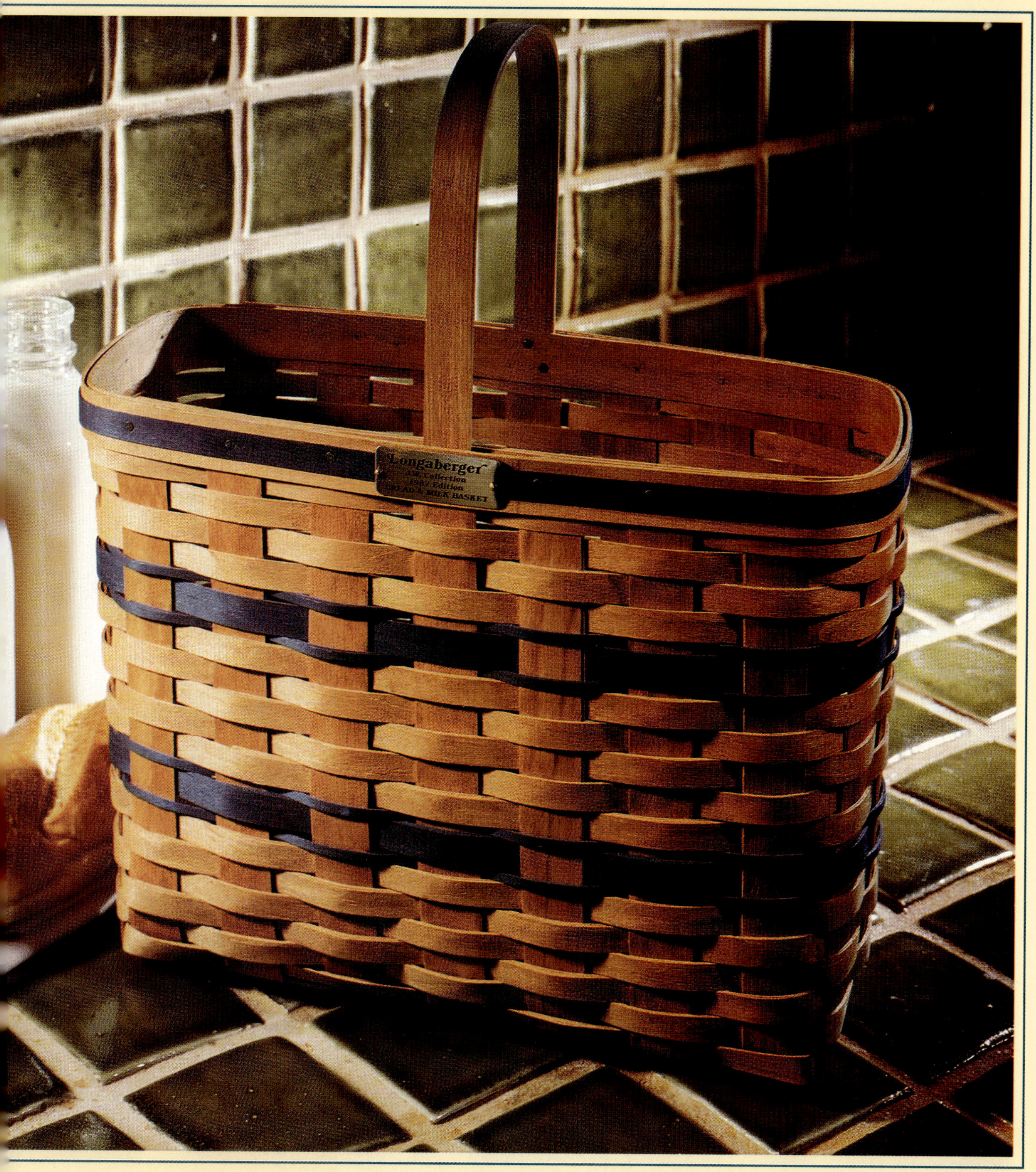
Longaberger
J.W. Collection
1987 Edition
BREAD & MILK BASKET

1988

GATHERING
BASKET

The Longaberger family had a large vegetable garden behind the house. Periodically, Bonnie, J.W. and the children would take their gathering baskets into the garden and place their just-picked produce into the baskets. Popular with Dresden families, the gathering basket was designed so it was narrow enough to fit between the rows of the garden, yet also long and deep enough to hold an ample amount of greens, carrots, or whatever else had ripened under the Ohio sun. Almost 50,000 of the 1988 edition were sold.

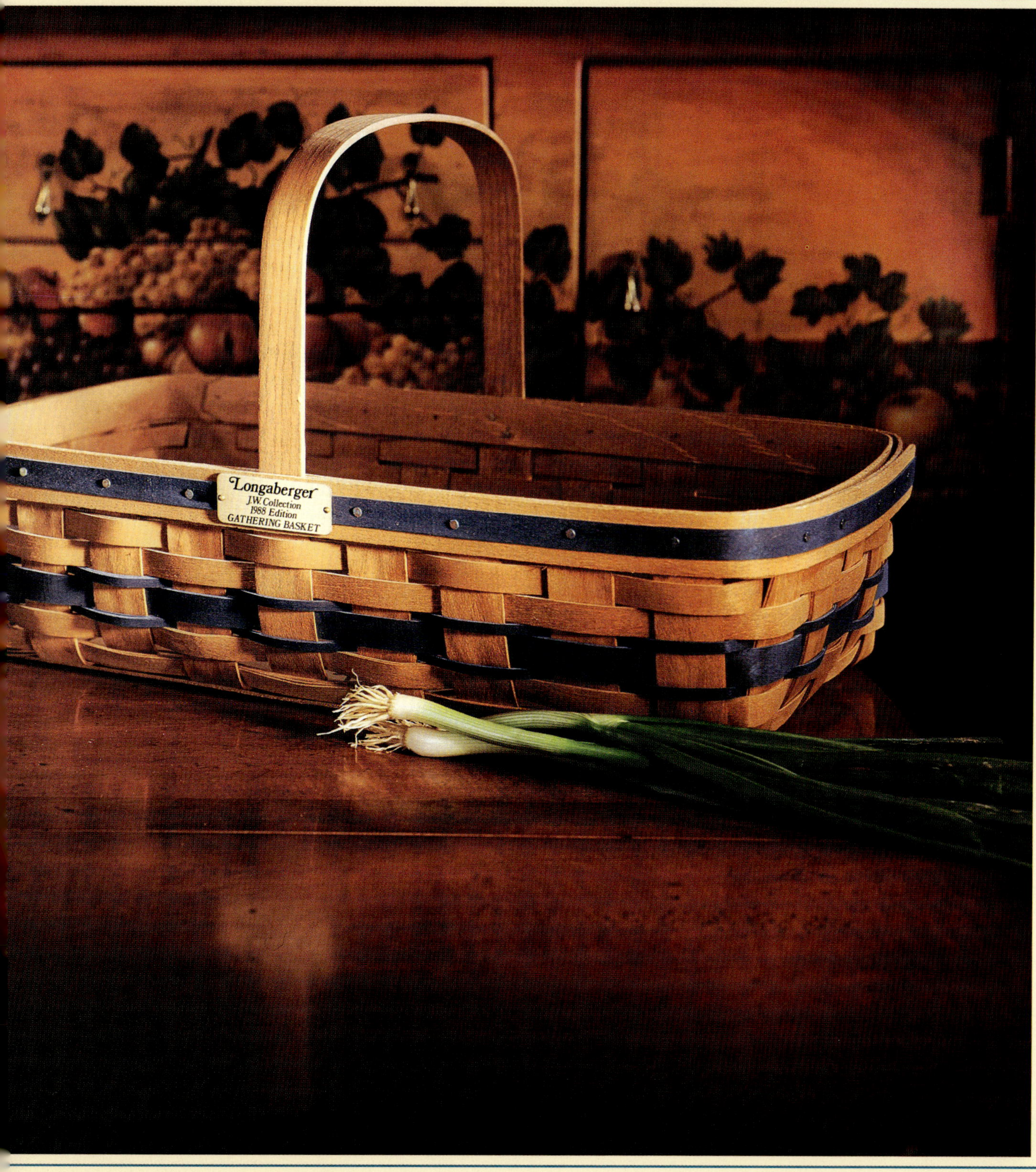
Longaberger
J.W. Collection
1988 Edition
GATHERING BASKET

1 9 8 9

BANKER'S WASTE BASKET

A J.W. design from the early 1940s became the seventh edition of the Collection. J.W. created his first banker's waste baskets for a friend who had asked for waste baskets that would serve their practical purpose, yet add to the decor of the local bank where he worked. Half a century later the originals, now on display at the Longaberger Museum, were still in use at the bank, and more than 53,000 J.W. Banker's Waste Baskets were sold.

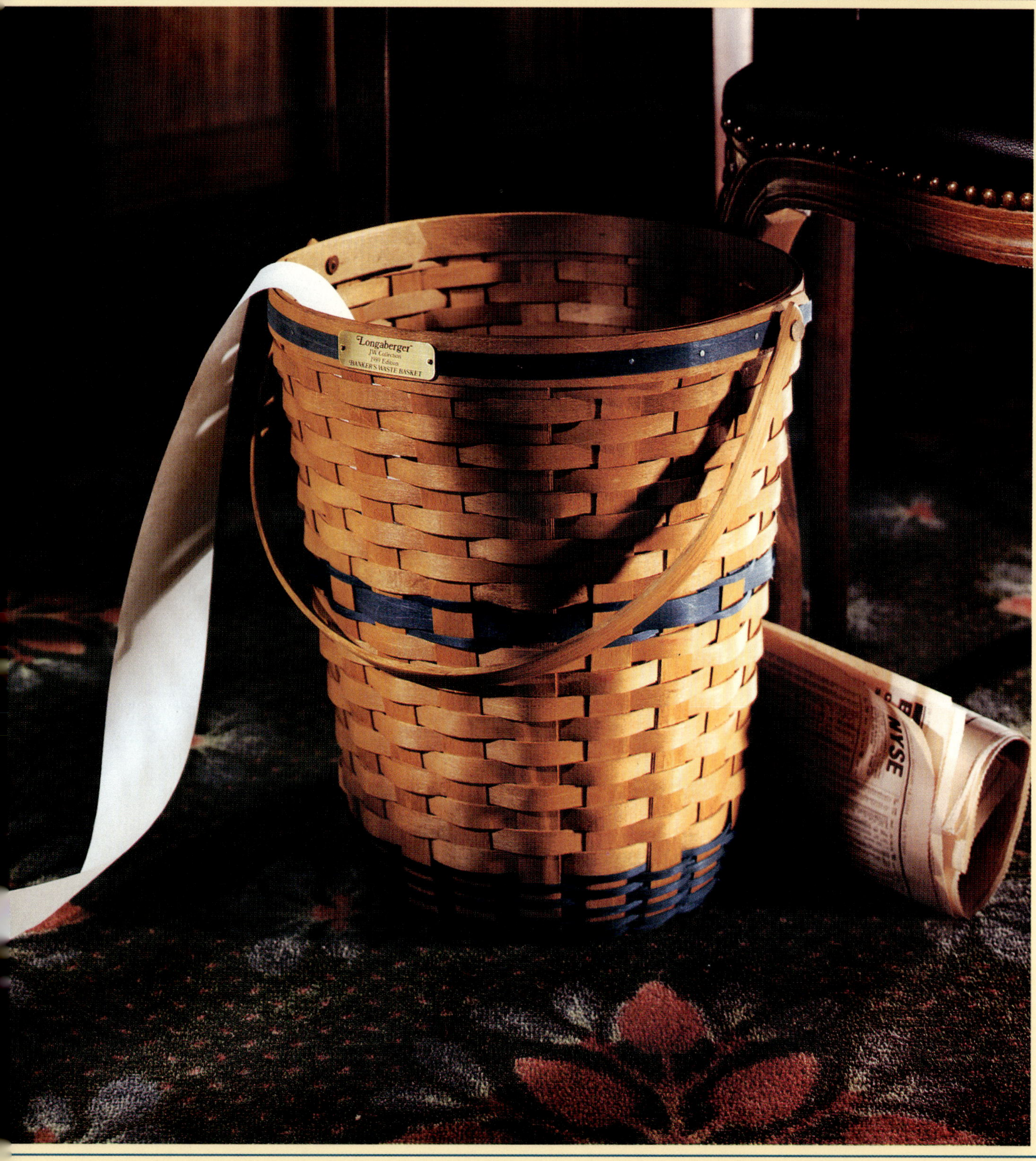
Longaberger
JW Collection
BANKER'S WASTE BASKET

1990

LARGE BERRY BASKET

*E*ach summer, the Longaberger children were sent to pick succulent berries from the bountiful bushes on "Machine Gun Hill," one of Dave's favorite childhood spots. Using leftover splints, J.W. created a basket especially for those berry-picking expeditions. His basket was big enough for a few pies worth of berries, but small enough for little hands to be able to carry easily. While the children may not always have enjoyed the work, they knew they would soon be enjoying the fruits of their labor. Some 37,000 people purchased the Collection's eighth edition.

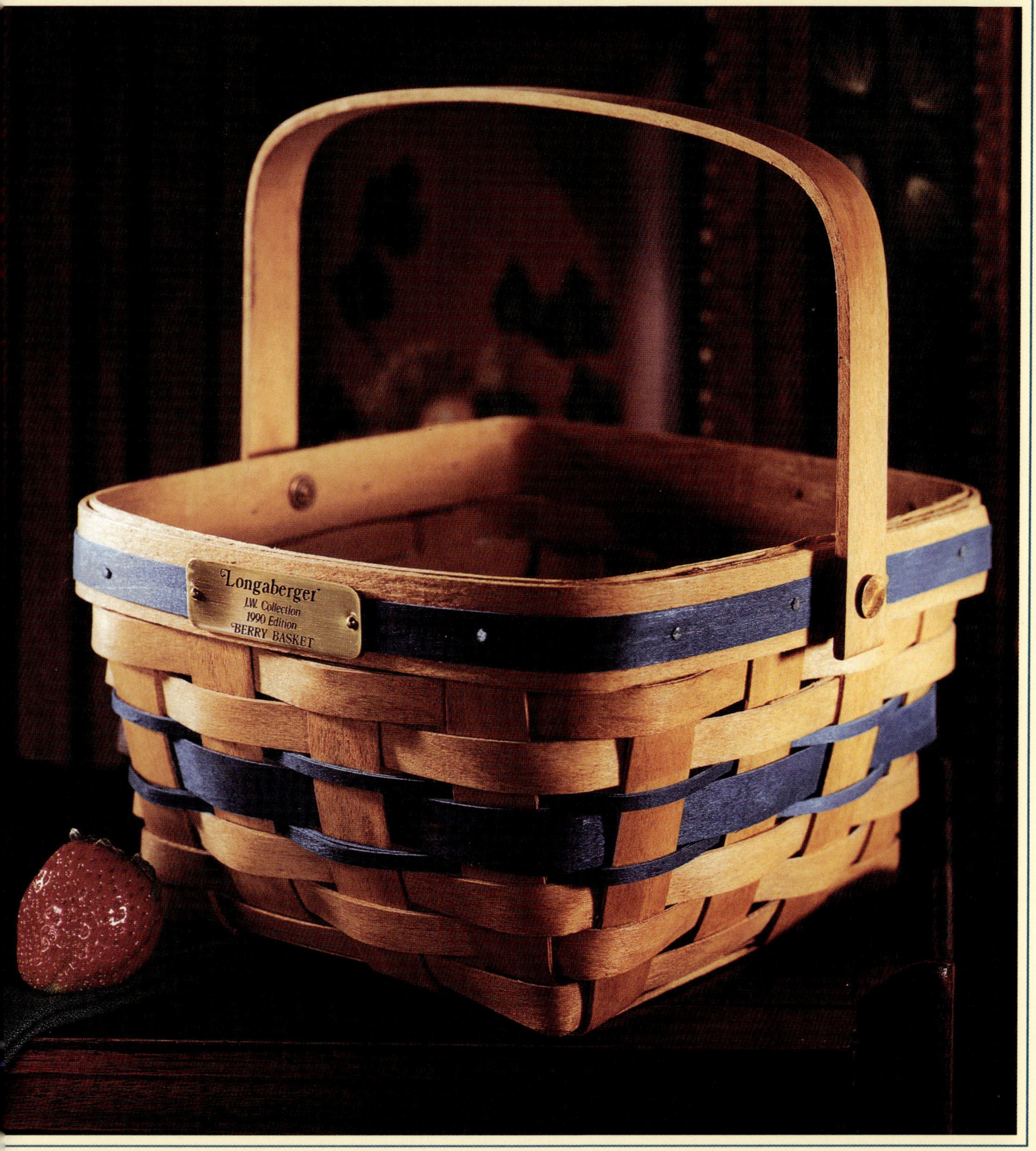

Longaberger
J.W. Collection
1990 Edition
BERRY BASKET

1 9 9 1

CORN
BASKET

Local farmers urged J.W. to create a basket that could withstand the rigors of harvesting. The outcome was a sturdy, bushel-sized basket that featured an inverted bottom with double upsplints and strong handles. Especially well suited for hauling corn from silo to feed wagon, J.W.'s corn basket also was used for many other tasks around both farm and home. The J.W. Corn Basket became the ninth edition of the Collection, and approximately 48,000 were purchased.

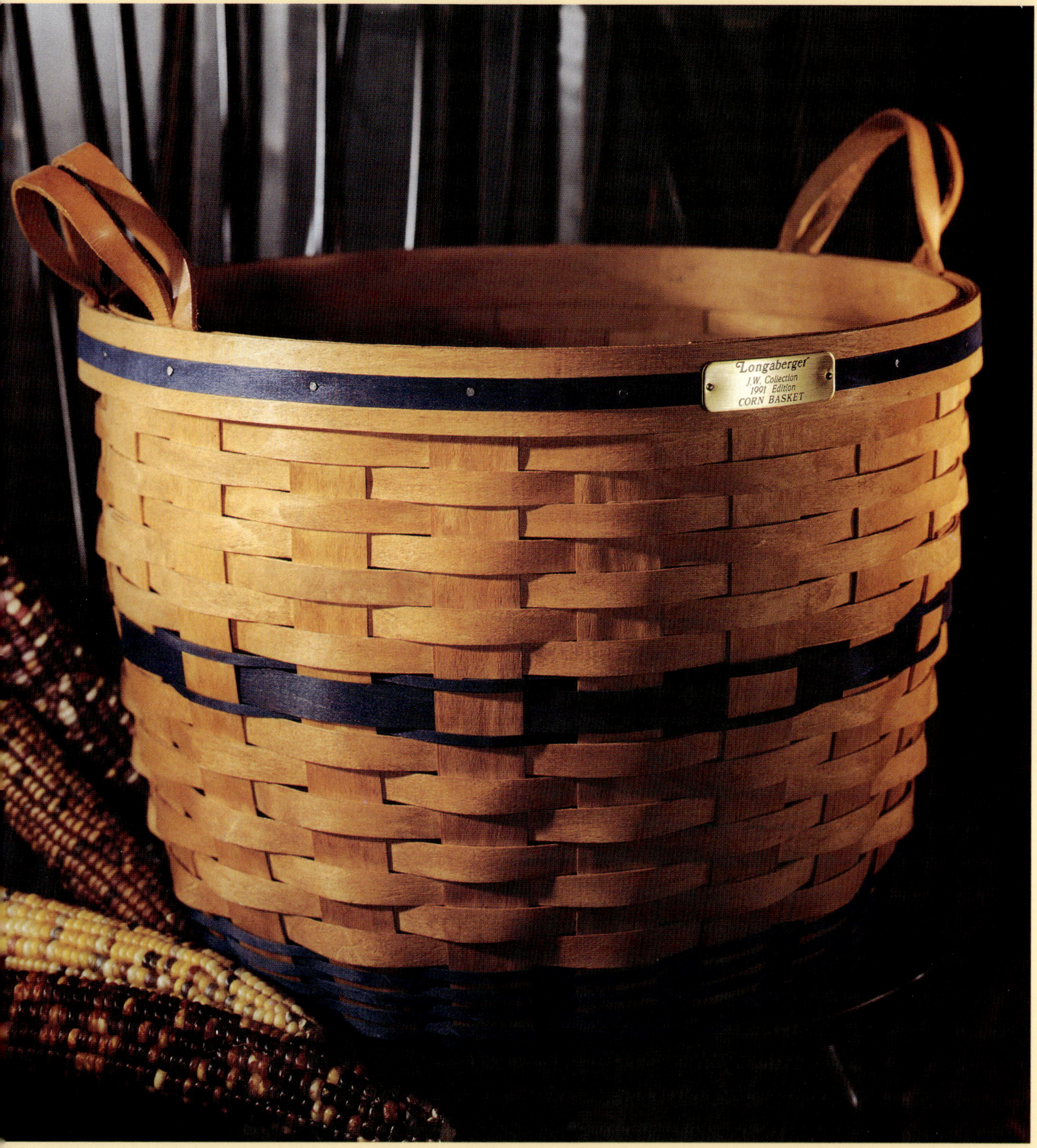
Longaberger
J.W. Collection
1991 Edition
CORN BASKET

1 9 9 2

CAKE
BASKET

When the folks of Dresden wanted to take a fresh-baked cake to a social function, they naturally reached for a cake basket made by J.W. His cake basket, Bonnie's favorite original, was 6 inches deep and 12 inches square; he often trimmed the top band or handle with braided rope. J.W.'s practical cake basket was quite popular around town in its day. The 1992 J.W. Cake Basket, with which Classic Plaid cloth accessories were introduced, was also very popular: More than 98,000 of them were purchased.

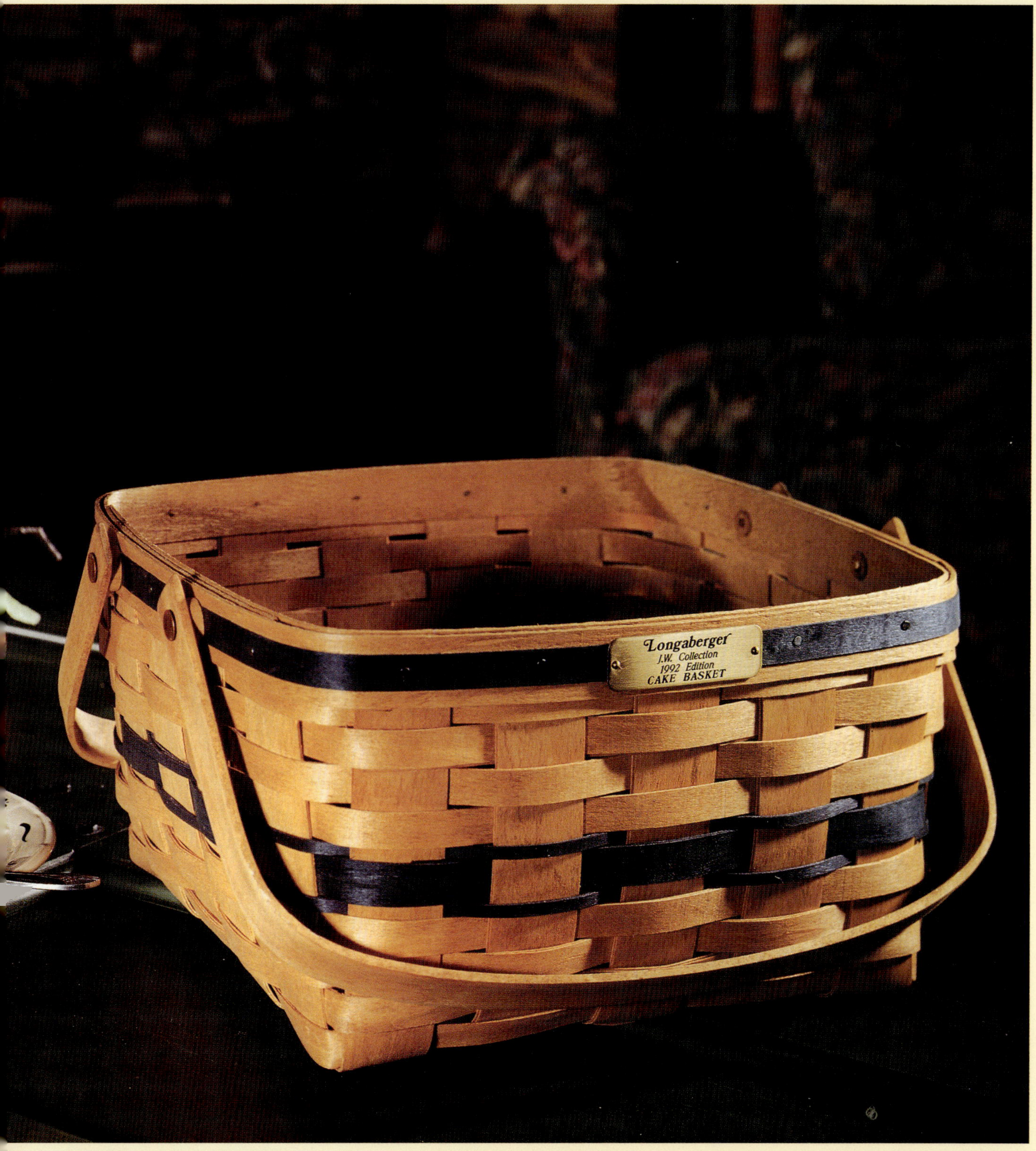
Longaberger
J.W. Collection
1992 Edition
CAKE BASKET

1 9 9 3

Easter
Basket

Each year, J.W. wove new Easter baskets for his children. Using clothing dye, he'd add bright color accents to match the dyed eggs Bonnie prepared. On Easter morning, all the children waited until everyone was awake before searching for the treat-filled baskets hidden in the yard. Of course, the first children to find the baskets enjoyed eating their candy while egging on the others. Approximately 77,000 collectors purchased this, the eleventh basket in the series.

Longaberger
J.W. Collection
1993 Edition
ORIGINAL EASTER BASKET

1994

UMBRELLA
BASKET

One of the most artistic of J.W.'s designs, the tall, sleek umbrella basket was made only on special request. Over the years the basket became known around Dresden as a handy storage receptacle for gladiola bulbs. The almost hourglass-shaped basket is cylindrical and stands 17-1/2 inches tall. It features a solid wooden bottom.

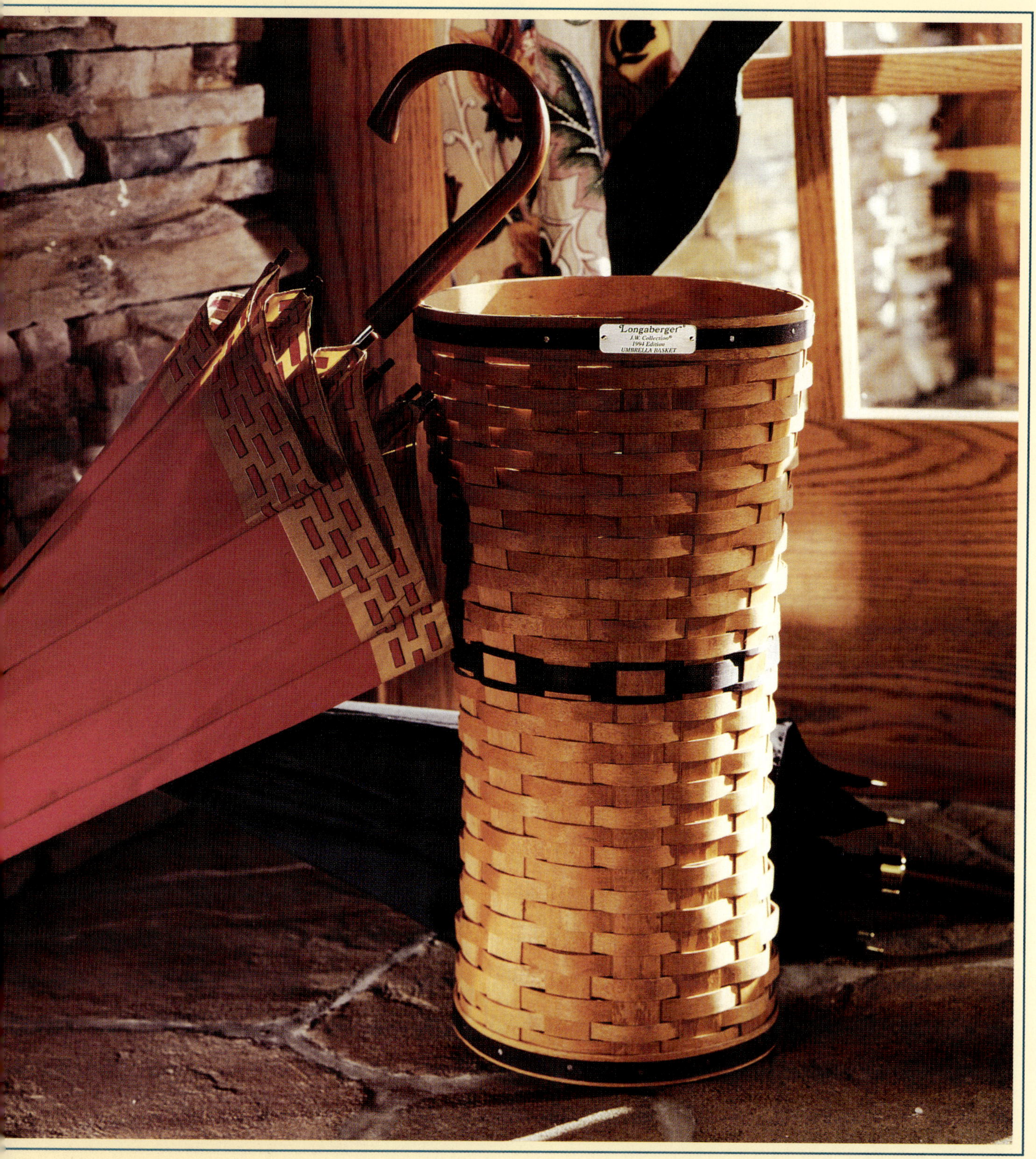
Longaberger®
J.W. Collection®
1994 Edition
UMBRELLA BASKET

Celebrating a legacy

When Dave introduced the J.W. Longaberger Collection in 1983, he envisioned a one-time offering of the Market Basket to commemorate his father's craft. But sales of the $32.95 basket far exceeded expectations, so the Company set out to make the Collection a premier series.

The decision was made to offer a different basket as part of the J.W. Longaberger Collection for a limited period each year until 1994. Each basket would be a J.W. original design, tagged and handsomely accented with weaves of Dresden blue, a popular color in the village's canal-era heyday and one that J.W. had often used.

Second in the Collection, 1984's Waste Basket cost $34.95, and sold less than the first. But realizing the relatively low sales would boost each basket's value over time, Longaberger's sales force promoted the Collection's investment potential. The claim that a basket bought today could later be worth enough to pay for a child's college tuition may have raised a few eyebrows at the time, but some baskets have already jumped to 20 times

Dave on the mezzanine of his Company's basket-making facility near Dresden.

their original value. As this secondary market emerged, collectors themselves set the worth of the baskets.

Sales of the Collection climbed fairly steadily for the next five years. The $45.95 Apple Basket of 1985 was outsold by the $34.95 Two-Pie Basket of 1986. A drop in sales with the $43.95 Bread and Milk Basket in 1987 was more than made up for by sales of the $36.95 Gathering Basket in 1988, a figure surpassed by sales of the $59.95 Banker's Waste Basket in 1989.

Sales fell with 1990's Large Berry Basket. But by then, advertisements in *Trading Post* (which lists items sold or traded by the Company's national family of Sales Associates) showed some baskets in the Collection were doubling in value in a year. Home-show customers had printed proof they were not just buying a basket—they were making an investment.

The 1991 Corn Basket outdid 1990's offering at nearly double the price. At $89.95, the Corn Basket was the largest in size in the Collection to date; its handsome, leather-loop handles make it one of the most attractive as well.

Offered for $55.95, the Cake Basket, Grandma Bonnie's favorite, sold well in 1992, the same year that *Classic Plaid*™ accessories were introduced. Two-sided fabric of 100 percent yarn-dyed cotton in a traditional, navy blue, burgundy and white plaid with the Collection's logo embroidered on one corner was presented as a liner for the basket, with complementing napkins also made available.

While true to J.W.'s design, 1993's $65.95 Easter Basket was made a little larger than his original. The change was done for the benefit of today's children, who generally receive more Easter goodies than did the youth of J.W.'s time. *Classic Plaid* accessories, including a pleated, drop-in liner, placemats and napkins, were offered.

The $74.95 Umbrella Basket of 1994, featuring a round, solid-maple bottom and a unique hourglass-shaped body, brought an exciting close to the J.W. Longaberger Collection, which over 12 years fulfilled all of its promise—and helped to raise the value of series such as the Christmas Collection, the All-American Series and the May Baskets.

Always at home in your home™

It's a typical day in America. A woman rises and pours fresh-brewed coffee into a Longaberger Mug. Taking the remote from a Bread Basket on the entertainment center, she flips on the morning news before watering her plants, which are potted in a variety of Measuring Baskets. Breakfast is served on Longaberger Dinnerware and as her children head off for school, their lunches are packed in Small Purse Baskets. As the woman sits at her desk, she pulls out a file from a Magazine Basket, then takes a pen from a Small Spoon Basket to write a letter to an old friend from college. Later, she's off for a teacher's retirement party with a Cake Basket full of cookies.

That evening, her spouse heats a casserole in a Longaberger Serving Bowl, while the children help her to load the car for the Longaberger home show she is conducting that night. The family sits down to dinner at a table set with Longaberger Baskets and Pottery. The events of the day are recounted as warm rolls are passed in a round Darning Basket.

The night's Longaberger home show is a great success: People love the baskets and the pottery. One guest asks about selling Longaberger products and the woman replies that, except for her family, the job is the best thing that ever happened to her. Freedom, flexibility, recognition and a career opportunity all became hers. And through her Longaberger business, she was able to foot the bill for her family's recent vacation.

For a quiet, unassuming man who left Ohio only once, whose entire world consisted of his family and the craft of basket weaving, J.W. Longaberger has had an extraordinary impact on American life.

Four generations of the Longaberger family:
(left to right, standing back) Tami (Kaido), Dave, Rachel (Schmidt); (seated center)
Mike, Matthew and Claire Kaido, Grandma Bonnie, Doug and Benjamin Schmidt;
(seated front) Dustin and Kaitlin Schmidt

Special thanks to the thousands of Longaberger Sales Associates and
employees who made this book possible.